ALL ABOUT MEASURING
WEIGHT

Julia Vogel

www.av2books.com

Go to www.av2books.com, and enter this book's unique code.

BOOK CODE

T429549

AV² by Weigl brings you media enhanced books that support active learning.

AV² provides enriched content that supplements and complements this book. Weigl's AV² books strive to create inspired learning and engage young minds in a total learning experience.

Your AV² Media Enhanced books come alive with...

Audio
Listen to sections of the book read aloud.

Video
Watch informative video clips.

Embedded Weblinks
Gain additional information for research.

Try This!
Complete activities and hands-on experiments.

Key Words
Study vocabulary, and complete a matching word activity.

Quizzes
Test your knowledge.

Slide Show
View images and captions, and prepare a presentation.

... and much, much more!

Published by AV² by Weigl
350 5th Avenue, 59th Floor New York, NY 10118
Website: www.av2books.com

Copyright ©2018 AV² by Weigl
All rights reserved. No part of this publication may be reproduced, stored in a retrieval system, or transmitted in any form or by any means, electronic, mechanical, photocopying, recording, or otherwise, without the prior written permission of Weigl Publishers Inc.

Library of Congress Control Number: 2016956740

ISBN 978-1-4896-5884-5 (hardcover)
ISBN 978-1-4896-5885-2 (softcover)
ISBN 978-1-4896-5886-9 (multi-user eBook)

Printed in the United States of America in Brainerd, Minnesota
1 2 3 4 5 6 7 8 9 0 20 19 18 17 16

122016
121616

Project Coordinator: Piper Whelan
Art Director: Terry Paulhus

Every reasonable effort has been made to trace ownership and to obtain permission to reprint copyright material. The publisher would be pleased to have any errors or omissions brought to its attention so that they may be corrected in subsequent printings.

The publisher acknowledges iStock and Shutterstock as the primary image suppliers for this title.

CONTENTS

2 AV² Book Code
4 Heavy or Light?
7 Gravity's Effect
8 Comparing Weights
10 Balancing Act
12 Ounces and Pounds
14 Tons and Tons
16 Metric System
18 Estimate It
20 Lots of Units
22 Measuring Mania
24 Key Words/Log on to www.av2books.com

Heavy or Light?

Who has the heaviest backpack?
Who has the lightest lunch?
Which book weighs the most?

How can you find the answers?
By measuring weight! Weight is
how heavy something or someone is.

You can weigh your backpack to see how heavy it is.

When you throw a ball in the air, gravity pulls it back down.

Gravity's Effect

What causes something or someone to be heavy or light? Earth has a force called gravity. Gravity pulls all things toward Earth. Weight is a measurement of Earth's gravity on objects.

You feel gravity whenever you jump up. No matter how hard you try to stay up, you come down! Gravity is stronger on heavier objects.

Comparing Weights

People haven't always had tools for measuring weight. Instead they measured weight by comparing two or more objects.

You can compare the weights of two books from your backpack. Hold one in each hand. Can you tell which one is heavier?

Gravity helps to move the ends of a seesaw up and down.

Balancing Act

A balance is a good tool for comparing weight. It works like a seesaw on the playground. What happens if a big brother sits on one end and his little sister sits on the other? The sister goes up. That is because gravity pulls the boy down more. He weighs more.

But if twins sit on each end, they balance. The twins weigh the same amount. The force of gravity is equal on each end.

Ounces and Pounds

A balance is good for comparing, but you can't find out how much something weighs. You have to use a scale for that. Many scales measure weight in the units of ounces and pounds.

Small, light things, such as a slice of bread, are measured in ounces. Sixteen ounces are in 1 pound. If you have a 1-pound loaf of bread and cut it into 16 equal slices, each slice weighs 1 ounce.

Types of Scales

What tool should you use to measure weight? That depends on what you're measuring. Spring scales are good for bags of apples at the store. Kitchen scales help measure how much chocolate to put into the candy you're making. Bathroom scales measure people's weights. Truck scales measure trucks, cars, and even elephants.

Spring Scale

Bathroom Scale

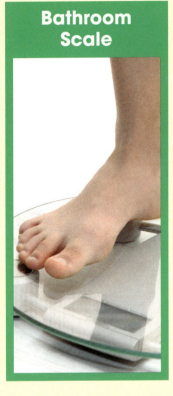

Kitchen Scale

Truck Scale

Tons and Tons

What if you had 200 bowling balls to weigh? They would be heavy—about 2,000 pounds. That's about as much as a small car!

For very heavy things, a different unit—the ton—is used. One ton is 2,000 pounds. That means 200 bowling balls weigh about 1 ton. How much would 600 bowling balls weigh? Three tons!

Metric System

People in the United States measure weight in ounces, pounds, and tons. These units are part of the U.S. customary system.

But most of the world uses the metric system. In the metric system, the basic unit for weight is the gram. A paper clip or a dollar bill weigh about 1 gram. Kilograms are used to weigh heavier things. One kilogram is 1,000 grams. A heavy schoolbook might weigh about 1 kilogram.

Today, cell phones usually weigh about 4.6 ounces (130 grams).

Metric Ton

There is a metric ton, too. One metric ton is 1,000 kilograms. A metric ton is not the same as a ton in the U.S. customary system. One U.S. ton is 907 kilograms.

Types of Scales

2 TALL Giraffes

1,555 Bouncy Basketballs

498 Red Bricks

412,357 Sweet Jelly Beans

1 BIG Polar Bear

You can guess which animal weighs more by looking at them.

Estimate It

What if you don't have a balance or a scale? You can estimate. To estimate a small object, hold something that you know weighs a few ounces, like a nickel, in one hand. Hold the object you're weighing in the other hand. Can you tell if one object is heavier? To estimate a heavy object, use your eyes. Does a rhino look heavier or lighter than a hippo?

You can use tools to check your estimates. For the small object, weigh it on a scale. For the heavy object, use the Internet. Look up how much a rhino and a hippo weigh to find out which weighs more. You'll learn a ton!

Lots of Units

Confused by all the different units for weight? Here's a list to help you keep them straight.

1 pound = 16 ounces

1 ton = 2,000 pounds

1 kilogram = 1,000 grams

1 metric ton = 1,000 kilograms

Adding with Units

Make sure you add measurements that have the same units. Two plus two does not equal four if you are adding tons and ounces. Remember to add pounds to pounds, ounces to ounces, and so on.

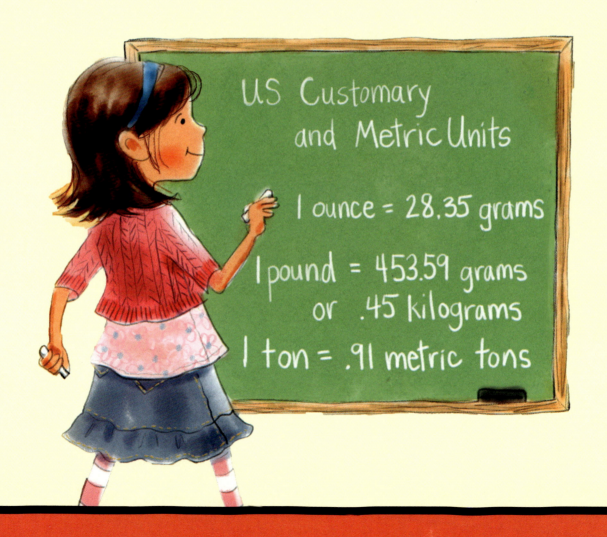

Measuring Mania

Now you can answer questions by weighing. You can tell in pounds and grams who has the heaviest backpack, the lightest lunch, and the weightiest books.

What other questions can you answer? Grab your scales and start measuring!

KEY WORDS

Research has shown that as much as 65 percent of all written material published in English is made up of 300 words. These 300 words cannot be taught using pictures or learned by sounding them out. They must be recognized by sight. This book contains 118 common sight words to help young readers improve their reading fluency and comprehension. This book also teaches young readers several important content words, such as proper nouns. These words are paired with pictures to aid in learning and improve understanding.

Page	Sight Words First Appearance
4	answer, book, by, can, find, has, how, is, most, or, something, the, which, who, you
5	it, see, to, your
6	a, back, down, in, when
7	all, be, come, Earth, hard, light, no, of, on, things, try, up, what
8	always, each, for, from, had, hand, more, one, people, tell, they, two
9	than, will
10	end, help, move
11	and, because, big, boy, but, good, he, his, if, like, little, other, same, that, work
12	are, as, cut, have, into, many, much, out, small, such, use
13	at, car, even, put, should
14	an, may
15	about, different, mean, three, very, would
16	air, might, part, these, world
17	not, there, too
18	them
19	does, don't, eyes, few, know, learn, look
20	here, keep, list
21	add, make, four, so
22	now, start

Page	Content Words First Appearance
4	backpack, lunch
6	ball, gravity
7	measurement, objects
8	tools
10	seesaw
11	balance, brother, playground, seesaw, sister, twins
12	bread, ounces, pounds, scales
13	apples, bathroom, candy, chocolate, elephants, kitchen, trucks
14	saltwater crocodile, ton
15	bowling balls
16	cell phone, dollar bill, gram, kilogram, metric system, paper clip, United States
17	basketballs, bricks, giraffes, jelly beans, metric ton, polar bear
19	dog, hippo, Internet, nickel, rhino

Check out www.av2books.com for activities, videos, audio clips, and more!

① Go to www.av2books.com.

② Enter book code.   T429549

③ Fuel your imagination online!

www.av2books.com